# The Salmon's Journey

Jon M. Fishman

Lerner Publications • Minneapolis

Lerner Publications Company
A division of Lerner Publishing Group, Inc.
241 First Avenue North
Minneapolis, MN 55401 USA

For reading levels and more information, look up this title at www.lernerbooks.com.


**Library of Congress Cataloging-in-Publication Data**

Names: Fishman, Jon M., author.
Title: The salmon's journey / Jon M. Fishman.
Description: Minneapolis : Lerner Publications, [2018] | Series: Lightning bolt books. Amazing migrators | Audience: Ages 6-9. | Audience: K to grade 3. | Includes bibliographical references and index.
Identifiers: LCCN 2017018463 (print) | LCCN 2017026528 (ebook) | ISBN 9781512498127 (eb pdf) | ISBN 9781512486377 (lb : alk. paper) | ISBN 9781541511835 (pb : alk. paper)
Subjects: LCSH: Salmon—Juvenile literature. | Salmon—Migration—Juvenile literature.
Classification: LCC QL638.S2 (ebook) | LCC QL638.S2 F57 2018 (print) | DDC 597.5/6—dc23

LC record available at https://lccn.loc.gov/2017018463

Manufactured in the United States of America
1-43461-33201-6/22/2017

# Table of Contents

# Meet the Salmon

*Splash!* A salmon jumps out of the water. Salmon are migrators. They move from one area to another at different times of their lives.

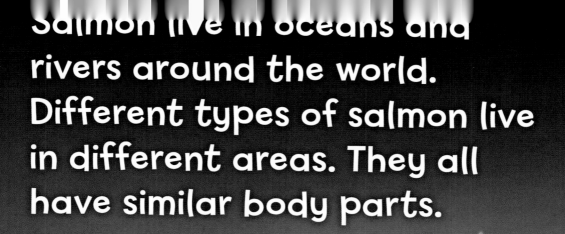

Salmon live in oceans and rivers around the world. Different types of salmon live in different areas. They all have similar body parts.

This is a pink salmon. Pink salmon mainly live in the North Pacific Ocean and nearby rivers.

A salmon paddles its tail near the surface of the water. Its strong tail fin pushes it ahead. Fins on its back, sides, and belly help it steer.

# A Salmon Hatches

A female salmon swims near the bottom of a river. She lays thousands of eggs in a nest in the rocks. Then a male salmon swims by to fertilize the eggs.

A salmon lays eggs in the fall. The eggs grow through the winter.

The eggs hatch in the spring. The baby fish are tiny. They are still attached to a part of their egg called the yolk. The little fish use the yolk for food.

Baby salmon stay in their nest for four to six weeks after they hatch.

The baby salmon are called fry when they leave their nest. Fry are between 1 and 2 inches (2.5 to 5 cm) long.

The fry eat insects and grow. They may stay in the river for one to two years. Some stay even longer. Then they begin their long journey to the ocean.

Young salmon have stripes on their sides. The stripes look like shadows and help the fry hide in the river.

# A Salmon Migrates

Something bright flashes below a river's surface. It's a salmon! The salmon's stripes have faded. Its scales are bright silver. It has grown large enough to migrate to the ocean.

A salmon's silver scales help it blend in with ocean water.

Salmon swim with the flow of the river. Soon they will reach the ocean. Salmon eat insects and other small animals on their trip.

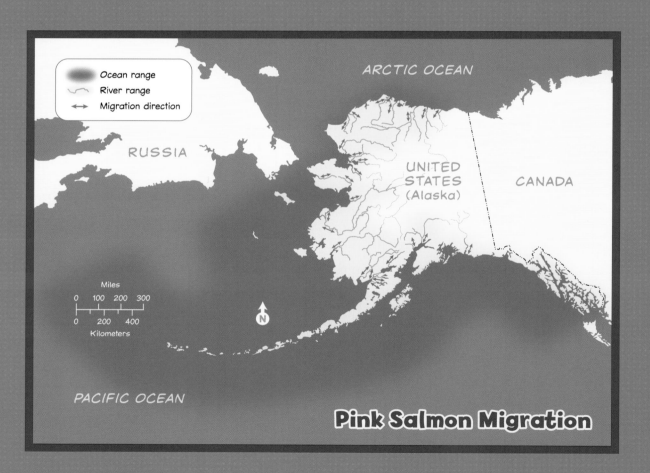

At first, salmon live in
groups in the ocean.
They stay near the shore.

A group of salmon is
called a school.

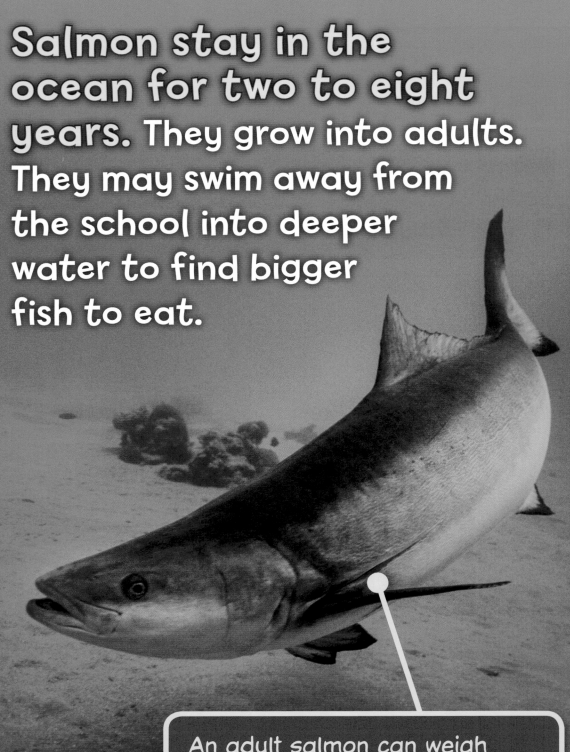

Salmon stay in the ocean for two to eight years. They grow into adults. They may swim away from the school into deeper water to find bigger fish to eat.

An adult salmon can weigh from 3 pounds (1.4 kg) to more than 100 pounds (45 kg)!

Salmon migrate back to the river where they hatched. They swim against the stream. They jump over waterfalls. Female salmon lay eggs in their home rivers to create more migrating salmon.

Salmon live for three to eight years.

# Salmon in Danger

*Chomp!* A grizzly bear tries to catch a migrating salmon. Bears and other predators eat salmon. Yet harm to the salmon's habitat is an even bigger danger.

on a warm day. The river was once a habitat for salmon. But farmers pumped water out of the river for their fields. Now the river is too shallow for salmon.

Trash and other waste in rivers can drive salmon away.

Salmon need clean, cold water. When people cut down plants that shade rivers from the sun, the water gets warmer.

Salmon have a harder time finding food and laying eggs in warm water.

Some people are working hard to protect salmon and their habitats. People may build fish ladders to help salmon get past waterfalls. Then the migrating fish can keep swimming from rivers to oceans and back again.

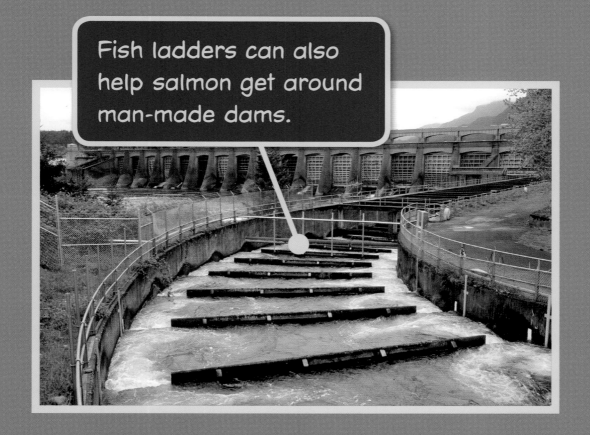

Fish ladders can also help salmon get around man-made dams.

# Fun Facts

- Salmon are known for their huge jumps when they travel up a river. The fish may be named after Latin words that mean "to leap."

- At one river in Scotland, salmon jump 12 feet (3.7 m) to get over a waterfall!

- Salmon meat is pink because of the food they eat. Wild salmon eat lots of small animals that turn their flesh dark pink. Salmon raised on a farm eat different food and are not as dark.

# More Amazing Migrators

- White sturgeon also migrate from rivers to oceans, but dams and other human activity have mostly ended their migration. These fish are common along the western coast of North America.

- Longfin eels hatch from eggs deep in the ocean. Then they travel to rivers in New Zealand. Near the end of their lives, these eels return to the ocean to lay eggs.

- The giant catfish in Asia is the world's biggest fish that doesn't live in oceans. It can be 10 feet (3 m) long and weigh about 650 pounds (295 kg). Giant catfish migrate up to 1,000 miles (1,609 km) to lay eggs.

# Glossary

**fertilize:** to cause eggs to grow a baby

**habitat:** the natural home of a plant or animal

**predator:** an animal that eats other animals

**scales:** the small plates that cover the outside of a fish

**school:** a group of fish

**shallow:** water that is not very deep

**yolk:** the yellow part of an egg that gives food to the baby

# Further Reading

Best, B. J. *Salmon*. New York: Cavendish Square, 2017.

Cleary, Brian P. *Catfish, Cod, Salmon, and Scrod: What Is a Fish?* Minneapolis: Millbrook Press, 2013.

Ducksters: Animal Migrations
http://www.ducksters.com/animals/animal_migrations.php

Easy Science for Kids: "Amazing World of Fish"
http://easyscienceforkids.com/all-about-fish

Eiler, John H., and Debbie S. Miller. *A King Salmon Journey*. Fairbanks: University of Alaska Press, 2014.

Salmon
http://pbskids.org/dragonflytv/show/salmonrun.html

# Index

# Photo Acknowledgments

The images in this book are used with the permission of: iStock.com/mit4711, p. 2; iStock.com/PerfectStills, p. 4; Design Pics Inc/Alamy Stock Photo, pp. 5, 9; iStock.com/dave iluck, p. 6; © Sergey Gorshkov/Minden Pictures, p. 7; Nature Picture Library/Alamy Stock Photo, p. 8; Thomas Kline/First Light/Getty Images, p. 10; iStock.com/eriktrampe, p. 11; © Laura Westlund/Independent Picture Service, p. 12; RugliG/Shutterstock.com, p. 13; Jeff Rotman/Photolibrary/Getty Images, p. 14; iStock.com/Bill_Dally, p. 15; iStock.com/ANDREYGUDKOV, p. 16; James Brunker/Alamy Stock Photo, p. 17; Thomas Kline/Design Pics/Getty Images, p. 18; Tim Matsui/RETIRED/Getty Images, p. 19; © Matthias Breiter/Minden Pictures, p. 22.

Cover: © Yva Momatiuk and John Eastcott/Minden Pictures.

Main body text set in Billy Infant regular 28/36. Typeface provided by SparkType.